ONE PERFECT BIRD

Sundress Publications • Knoxville, TN

Published by Sundress Publications

Editor: Erin Elizabeth Smith
erin@sundresspublications.com
http://www.sundresspublications.com

ISBN: 0-9723224-8-5

Colophon: This book is set in Liberation Serif.

Cover Image: Eleanor Leonne Bennett

Cover Design: Rhonda Lott

Book Design: Erin Elizabeth Smith & T.A. Noonan

ONE PERFECT BIRD

Letitia Trent

ACKNOWLEDGMENTS

42 Opus: Whee!
The Bedside Guide to No Tell Motel - Second Floor: Song
Black Warrior Review: Landscape
Crossconnect: Eurydice in the Underworld
Dusie: The Births, Biography of Flax
The Denver Quarterly: Dream Boat
Juked: The animal I made you, Advice from the I-Ching on what to write about next
Mipoesias: Schooling, Love Poem
Ocho: I reach my hand inside his cranium
Pebble Lake Review: Yellow
Poemelon: Give
POOL: Varieties of Ghost, Outbound, Fairy Tale Pattern

The poems “If You See Kay”, “The Jackpot” and “Congratulations” appeared in the chapbook *The Medical Diaries.*

TABLE OF CONTENTS

Outbound

We are boarding the slim
silver train, trailing sweet

expectations like Swedish Fish
from the little girl's fist.
          Look, she says, and I lower
my head: a red
palm, jelly in her teeth.

Suddenly everyone is moving, wheeling
squeaky suitcases, brushing pretzel pieces
from their button catches or tiny vest pockets.   Look,

I say, we've got to go, got
     to get moving. Her fish trail us

like footprints, like where we've
come from jellied and risen to follow.

The conductor is in silver and the hum of
machinery rises like rust
       in a wheel-well—slow

then all of a sudden. You'll have to ride
all sticky, I say, meaning to make her understand, to make

her weep, you'll have to ride like a dirty living
letter in a good, clean envelope.

Schooling

I excelled at many lessons
they taught us: like drowning,
for instance. I could fit an entire banana
down my throat without choking.
I never could shimmy up that rope,
though, no matter how much Fresh Prince
the gym teacher blasted. But this

was a small failure, like those cheap
pencils that slip right off the slick
brown paper. *Mama had a baby and his*
head popped off, and, I swear to God,
Jordan's nose spat like a busted faucet.
But back to the major lessons—
What's in Your Pants? And
Animals in the Classroom.

I excelled at keeping Mister
Caramel watered and rested.
Though Jordan told me that he'd kiss me
if we freed the hamster, and I did—Mr. Caramel
ran right for the closest busted
hole in the plaster. I don't even
want to imagine what happened
after Daddy installed that whiskey
bathtub and mom whipped up
a batch of furious bacon. I excelled

the very most at drowning, and Susie
at cartwheels, and everyone but
Gregory made granny knots

during camping field trips. The trick
is to imagine being a stone that wants
to burrow into the soft silt underwater.

You've got to really want it, the coach
said, metal whistle clicking between
his teeth. Mom echoed his gesture
at the dinner table—*You've learned
to open your throat completely,* she said,
spearing her gristle, *I never did.*

Orange

Nobody's favorite, it's the Popsicle left
behind after the others—purple, red, even lime,
the color of school tile. I've seen

orange hands in internet photographs
from too many carrots, a vegetable that riots,
electric, though we can no longer see

its strangeness. Were the first farmers shaken,
you think, at that shock of fluorescence?
I learned early that orange isn't calm—it's

embalming fluid, the rings around Saturn,
chameleons during arousal or aggression.
                    Return to your first

memory of color: Big Bird's feathers
like emery board against your eyes;
the grey soup of television, that condensed

confusion, more terrifying than any
children's toy come to life wielding his
tiny knife, his sweater's stripes—but not worse

than the shock of orange hair above his
always thumbed-open eyes.
                                        And in *Poltergeist,*
the blonde's nose-to-nose with an orangeless

fizz, a ghost soda that even Christ can't fix,
though the housing development is all greys
and blues and cools.

Don't worry, mother said,

come to bed. The kiss stuck to my forehead
every time she left was a heart of burnt brick,
corroded tailpipe, the copper of the fields where

we came from come September—all a darker strange
than the peel under my fingernails, the silty *Tang*
in our cups, the color of the hunters' vests

like ribbons through the birches as they searched
our forest for any rusty bursts of blood.

Yellow

Nothing remains
but the color. The dress

was yellow, that much
is certain, and now sun

crowds the mouth and covers
the hands like mittens.

The memory has always been
spotty and pocks dot

what's left of the image—
caramel-salt, tan as postcard sand,

a scrape of grain under
the tongue. Somebody tall

has that hand. His fist fits right
around it. Nothing remains

but the metal purse-clasp
banging the hip. Like zipping

fingernails along a screen door,
the little peals

multiplying. The movie called
yellow runs back, but only so—

then sticks in the gears. An old-
time film projector on fire,

film cracking black oil bubbles,
all the faces running off.

All that remains is the color
yellow, that much is certain.

It's in the attic, or closet,
or photographs and somebody wants

to say, but can't, that it still has
a soapy, steel-wool smell about it.

Varieties of Ghost

1.

Banging around in our
        shifty foundation.
Folding its shoulders to slide

up through the quiet toilet.
Whipping the mousetrap

in the matchbook alley between
          the counter and refrigerator.
Stippling our skin when it passes.

2.

The whole scene is done up
in turquoise, just like grandma
        in our memory
paying bills at the kitchen table.

Just like eye shadow during certain decades.
Just like a moony dusting of glitter.

3.

It lingers like apple core under
the flip-up desk top. Lingers

like that mean letter you crayoned
to mother. After you lost her,

you found it folded with her issues
of *The Weekly World News*
and her Sunday morning lapel pins.

4.

Even the last arrangement
of umbrellas in the wide-mouthed

wicker basket bears some
half-birthed significance.

The dusty cupboards are pregnant
with salt and crackers sopping

the leavings. You remember
the texture when a shriveled leaf

rakes your palm. You remember
the smell of mother coming in

from winter when you strip
the pine cone's scales—menthol

and stinging pockets of cold air.

Whee!

She's in lace-edged socks and holds a berry-picking
basket. A prudent voice like the weatherman:

Better bring an umbrella. Better mind the skyline
during your long drive. She eats sugar by the handfuls

straight from the bag. She can only imagine cars
on the highway. Thinks they must glint like boats

on a blue harbor. She can only imagine boats
on a blue harbor. She doesn't drive. Can't fill out

her forms without me—*Who is our emergency contact?*
Where do we live now? Once she held a spatula

against the flame until it caught the curtains,
then her dress, then her flesh. What a mess

that was. I entertained the reaper while he waited at our
crumb-strewn table, bones around a coffee cup, for her

to burn down to a manageable puddle. I exaggerate.
But you're dripping wet! Did you forget your umbrella?

Fairy Tale Pattern

A king hovers
at the narrative's edge
or stands

at the center giving orders
and daughters. It's sometimes
necessary to let the tame bear
rip his belly open, the dwarf-on-call

chop his head off. It's all
a matter of equilibrium

and the moral demands a smooth
transition of power. Those on high
must learn their lessons

by scrubbing tiles. Then,
they must be dressed in red
again and extricated
from dangerous marriages (see

"The Robber Bridegroom,"
his cauldron of calves, a whole

princess liver dinner). We sigh
at the end because of all
that has passed. So many shoes

danced through. So many suitors
slaughtered. We keep reading.
Next page: another princess gives birth

to two beautiful daughters.
She’s in the paragraph and has
no perspective on the matter.

We want to tell her: just let the blue lights wander.
Let the snake slick in their bowl of milk.

Another one about the material

Here's what I love: the idea
that *stuff* is voluble—
that leaves unfurl a face,

mustachioed,
in the cup's wet dregs,
that the duchess and death
have something on me.

My absence is Finnish-chinned
and fair, or so the blonde
leaves say. The cards
keep quiet while cups

click in the cupboards,
tickled by old whisker prints.

The air is no longer smoke
that I chew like oats,
but a conversation

between three voices. Mine, his,
and the photographs we're stopped in
and can't remember. The immaterial

tints like smell, like music.
I've decided that the air
is not empty and so

it has happened: he speaks
to me through frames

and forks lined straight
on picnic tables. I can’t

even sleep sometimes just thinking
of the racket if the silverware

decided to tell everything
that has happened.

Vision

Hold still, the optometrist says,
    and her light knifes
the spread pools. My eye's veins

    black-branch across
a ballooning dome. It lets
      everything in, she says,

did you notice a change
      in vision? Her light, secured
to her forehead, darts

 across my chest. A loss
     of precision, perhaps? Look
to the left, then look

     to the right.
                        The bare crisscross
above me when I lie back
      on the snow's breast. The real

 bone-fingered backdrop
          framing every merry
sleigh-ride Christmas card.
                                        The eye,

        she says, bumping my knee,
shattering the dome, is a surprisingly
       complicated organ. That dark-

filled hole. That bright band
     of muscle. The cones. The whole
dead forest swelling inside it.

Makeover

I think we got exactly what we wanted,
though not in the shape we expected,
not in any form we recognized. Our hearts

had hoped for platinum boxes flanked
by wide-winged angels, or skulls
with the caps hinged off, inlaid in velvet.

Something classic yet also modern,
like marrying four women or dances
ending in burst blood vessels. They brought

it in tablets to split between our teeth.
They claimed it traveled better through blood,
not rumor. Admittedly, we were suspicious.

Then it happened. Music blew through
our remembered rooms. We'd expected tidying,
yes, but not a complete overhaul, a total

redo. The whole town smelled like
thinner and chambray work-shirts, and we,
having nowhere to sleep, became acquainted

with doorsteps and public kitchens.
Now we can't help but smile at each other,
recognizing the same stiff walk, the same red cheek.

I think we've gotten what we wanted.
And when we run our hands along the walls
the smudges are like ghosts on our palms.

Advice from the I-Ching on what to write about next

You are unable to move at the moment. You're holding two heavy-duty trash bags bursting with wheat pennies. You'd meant to carry them to the coin acceptor but stopped mid-street, sensing the onset of metaphor. Don't worry. You will be relieved before furrows of rips stitch along your inner arm. You might just drop the bag or let the strained plastic slit. You look at the omens in the sky. Not just jets scribbling smoke—even more unlikely. Something like a solid block of human waste falling through a ceiling, for instance. You see such extraordinary sights that you are unable to respond. You try to speak of them, but only the smell of copper drifts from your throat. You cannot even think to set the pennies down. Don't worry. You hear horns and skids whistling distant past you. You will be relieved or you will not be relieved. Try not to cry about it. This is not a mistake.

Advice from the I-Ching on whether I should take up public speaking

Draw back
and contemplate.
The swelling soup
blooms against the bowl's
lip before it slips. Take
no action yet. Heavenly
bodies persist, forever
whipping the same orbit.
Withdraw. Inside
the biggest doll nest
dolls smaller and smaller,
the tiniest most likely
to be pocketed by a child.
Like it, be smallest.
Conceal. Make
no choices yet.

Variation on the Twelve Dancing Princesses

A tree cracked with a loud report.
A great lake, whereon stood
twelve little boats, each one
more beautiful than the other.
"Just trod a little on her dress:
you'll be invisible." He let the wine
run down, opened wardrobes,
cupboards. "You are a goose who
is always frightened." They saw
that they were betrayed and
brought out tokens. When all
the shoes were danced into holes,
no one could figure out how
it had happened; they slept together
in one chamber, each more
beautiful than the other. You can
steal after them, she said, they're
silver and they shine and glisten.
He reached the door just before
them and bolted it shut behind him.

The Reader's Digest Guide to North American Wildlife

With Flowers

Blankets of bluets. At each fork
in the stem, a whorl of leaves.
We called them forget-me-nots

never knowing their names. Called them
bluebells, called them milk weed. Small flowers
rise from the centers of the whorls.

And buttercups: beggars once used them
to induce sores on their faces. But mother
held them to my chin *butter skin*

if you're in love! I always was.
Bundles of bluets burst one morning
while we slept and at the sight

I dropped my bucket. The bee's tongue strikes
a plate within a freshly opened
flower. Twist bundles to bring

to mother, her hands open. They quickly
carpet newly cultivated ground from coast
to coast. *These ones are weeds*, she said,

tossing them in the garbage, putting the good
ones, the flowers, in aspirin-clouded

water. Children sucking out the nectar
have been known to be poisoned.

Birches

Birches are a special delight
in winter, adding texture
to a snowy forest, and in summer
separating us from the Johnsons,
their pool deck and lotion-slick
daughters rattling magazine
inserts, earrings dangling
clusters of flowers open
and releasing pollen.
Sometimes I heard
the silvery bark of their golden retriever
and distant laughter, usually female
flowers develop slim, white
wrists, clanking bracelets
like branches with black
vertical cracks. Their twigs
had a wintergreen odor
of smoked meat and firecrackers.
The birches caught
the arc of fire and burst into flames
of yellow and orange in autumn:
tweeds and heathers, pleats
and knee socks up the thigh.
We stood at opposite
bus stop sides. The ones who remain
are called losers, skanks, or
survivors, breeds that keep
shade for later woodland invaders,
the ones that stay rooted
to die at an early age.

Selfheal/Healall

The cup bottoms up
and fire soaks the softness
along her arm. Colonists brewed
a bracing tea and its influence
on cats is a strange side

effect, like scars in little squares
on the inner arm and gauze
scattered along
the lawn. Clusters of healalls,
their dew sore-scalding
by old wives'

estimations. Unwilling to let
the doctor probe she screamed
until the daisies dwindled. Lollipopless,
the doctor wrapped her. Healalls are the first
to appear, sometimes warming

up from under a snowfall.
The doctor kept scribbling
prescriptions. They collected
them as makeshift coasters
for bologna sandwich picnics

on beds of brown-eyed susans. *You're*
improving. Selfheals are
related to healalls how? Both petals
taste like medicine
or poison and the name comes
from the yawning throat

of the flowers. Sleep: the selfheal,
healall, and not the dew-taste
silvercupped in its buds.

Molt

Like others, it molts
several times a season,
though most do it all
at once and not in pieces.

When ready, it loses
all interest in eating.
Its eyes close, indicating
new tissue is forming.

Until clear, it stays coiled
in hiding, sluggish, colder
than the rock chips, the mud
dips where the body slid.

It's hiding. It knows
it's ready when the skin
of its head begins to split.

Then it slicks through
cropping rock to pull
the loose off, inside out,
like a wet sock.

Biography of Flax

Big-headed, blue
          and hirsute. The Romans
     called them linum, and the Egyptians
fashioned mummy wraps and
          ancient fibrous fishnets. Oh, and linoleum
   came from the oil slicking between its blue-
 wrapped seeds. A plant upon which
             civilization was built, it tips
      toward the puddle, leaves
 mud-edged, and the startled
caterpillar knuckles in its cup.

Martial Fervor

What to look for:
        rolled-over effigies; the rubble
                of spotlights on pocks; sterile
frostbite moving plumelike;
       a casket-sparse,
           vaudeville-shaped coalition; all blue
                                        and erect in Wisconsin.

The Births

Births are a special delight
        in Wisconsin:
their decorative baroques, their colostrums and
        Thanksgivings before a snowy witness.

Many births are pioneer tremors—
                spectacles that grow in soil
                    exposed by fishhooks, flukes

        that open
            and release
         ghosts in torrents.

After pregnancy,
the female fluidity
becomes a solid confection.

Love Poem

You're not a dog at all.
Daily, you sleep in slight depressions.
Your warning is a headstand.
You express yourself through screams, chirps and whistles.
During the fall you become restless and aggressive.
You eat anything of the proper size, whether dead or alive.
Your kits are the size of bumblebees.

You truly seem to enjoy life.

Not surprisingly,
another one of your names is *glutton.*
You live on tender shoots and ripe grain.
Your long ears act as antennae and air conditioners.
You have well-formed, almost human hands.

Anger as an Animal

A tiny bundle of furious
energy, it lives solitary, wedges
its spindle-shaped body through
the sod like swimming, searches
frantically for food, eats twice
its weight a day,
and cannot truly fly—it glides
downward and downward and bounces
off objects, returning
as an echo.

Snow Plant

No hummingbirds, those crazy-
hearted stars of nature documentaries,
or bee-clouds hovering above

a whole heavy-headed row.
It calls carrion creatures, clawed beetles,
backs black as men's dress shoes.

And the plant, like raw meat
dropped on the ground. One doesn't ask
about intention for forget-me-nots

or firewheels. But this smells of salt
and the copper tint of liver. Imagine:
a bouquet of skinned fingers.

But it's a flower because its petals
pile over a pipe of flesh-stem rooted
in humus, red as cardinal crowns,

red as cheeks on Christmas. Never
tipping up to eat the light, it draws what
cuts in the dark. It draws the crows

to root its folds, draws the beetles
for burying seed.

Musk Wraith

Contrary to folklore
they don't shoulder
the earbones
of sleeping people.

The musk wraith
is full of survival. Dig a tunnel,
line it in silk, and seal
the entrance.

These insomniacs
have an elaborate
social origami. Some shoot up
right before your very faces.

Few of the species
are poisonous to humans.
Their organs differ
microscopically: only females
have a sharp, barbed,
usually hollow mouthpiece.

Four Seasons

I.

Beekeepers are primarily
poltergeists; mesh net masks
and subtly singing beards,
bee bodies slipping from
their chins like honey.

II.

Twelve black perambulators
parked along the walkway
watch her ponytail's wispy, winged
arc. She releases her sticky
fingers from the chain and lands
on her sandals and hands.

III.

Mother's jolt-choked
and holds her fist to breastbone
when the child runs through
bright leaves releasing blood
from her knees and palms
like bees from an old juice cup.

IV.

Winter is manufactured by
the fuel of spectators. They weigh
their bodies in sweaters. Their cheeks

frost like ice grapes. Outside, a squall
settles along the toothy sunset.
Balled inside this squall, needlework
attracts annihilation.

The animal I made you

has a long tail with no
known function. It shoulders
a swollen egg-laying apparatus.
It springs, landing on its
hard, burrowing claws.

It has transparent, almost veinless wings,
useless, as to be expected. It sees you
with its two protuberant eyes and tries
to create a basket-like trap with its legs
over and over until exhausted. I failed it
by cutting corners, neglecting

the wasp-waist, the armor plates,
and that noisy, yet effective,
closed circulatory system.

Song

None of the doors I want
to enter open.

Olive eyes, red-flecked,
ogle in their jars,
hug the panty blush
of always summer.

He starts packing
in anticipation.

The water heater grumbles
in its dusty cupboard and
the cat won't even brush
her thrumming ribs against it.

He just starts stripping
the faux-brick wallpaper.

Out on the lawn he decides
he loves me and unbuttons
me down to the navel.

I puncture the plastic
and a waterfall of translucent
lids spills down the counter.

Spring shimmies through
the mini-blind slats. Yellow
paint blotches all our cottons.

We carry it everywhere.

The smell is clean, it’s true
but also mean. And also sour.

Dream Boat

He wants shoes that slip easy on his feet,
and when he says *I want shoes* he wants them
pointing faithfully, like a dog's two paws
with the head lowered between. He wants a dry
toothbrush. To him, Easter should be accompanied
by tympanis and clarinet recitals
by enthusiastic children. He specifies
split reeds and cherry cola. He secretly wants
one at home, spilling peanuts on the counter.
He wants me with a whip, the tip of my pump
against his coccyx. Do you suspect that he's bodiless?
The only question is what he means as a symbol.
And how even the unconscious, like a rigged
shopping cart, pulls a hard right toward
the brightest produce. We could watch him
from a distance swimming laps around
the kidney-shaped pool, initial-embroidered towel
whipping his thighs after he comes clean from the blue.
Chip, Kit, Logan, Gatsby, every boy who bestows
his friends with sun and pool house loss
of innocence. But I want him to say something
redeeming, revealing that we both watch for signs
of light across the lake and we are both piled bright
silk shirts and we are both traveling across
the blue in exhausted little boats.

A Romantic Encounter

Following the phrase "silently
disrobing," a typographical
error appears—keep moving
your eye down the slide
of sheer and sheerer clothing.
It says "he bends to kick the rosy
bud of her breast": what's meant
is "*kiss* the rosy bud." Don't let
the image erupt on the onion
skin. Page twenty seven, he's
putting his pants back on, lacing
his belt through the loops,
rooting for his far-flung
shoes. She just happens to have
a pack of cigarettes that
she doesn't open, fearing
the predestination of films
and sleazy scenes like this one
where the man observes how much
he likes to see the woman post-
fuck disheveled, eyelashes
on her chin, and she thinks she might
like a bacon and tomato sandwich.
Then a mood, like a sick smell
leaking through the badly caulked
glass, colors the book's slick
pages. He asks her to get off
her ass and open up the window,
can't she see he's suffocating,
and the page ends on the word *glitter.*

If You See Kay

There are things that can be accomplished only
by violence. Physical love is unthinkable without violence.
-Milan Kundera

Don't believe the false etymologies (for example: it wasn't
carved—
For Unlawful Carnal Knowledge—
above the pink-blotched adulterers at the stocks,
kneeled in their favorite position, heads
finally separated from their bodies,
officially, before God and everybody)—

it's just a word
for hit, strike, pierce, punch,
penetrate, in Germanic plosives
and fricatives, and variations on uh
or ohh or even ahh or eeee;

Grimm's law and a juggling of soft,
pliable vowels are the only
true stories, and your mouth around
the spiky consonants

is the reason you can't help
but spit when you say it.

Russian Snowball

Russian. Tongue click. *You look Russian.* I touch my hair. My license clicks down *snap.* His jacket ripples like pinched skin. Cigars sit in full, dusty boxes. Wrapped in plastic, women whip their hair. They kneel on heels, flat-skinned and pliant. He shouldn't watch me watching, so I turn from them. Bottles click in their paper when I bump against them. *Stupid knuckles*—he steadies the receipt as I loop my name. *You could be from my country*; I smile and he returns it. Only bigger, with a slip of something caught between his teeth, an impression. The women behind him pose in rows, glad eyeing past the glossy limit. There is no resemblance, and he shouldn't watch me watching, so I turn from them. Goodbye floats behind me as I open the door for a woman, hands full already. For a moment my breath burns unexpected—in the close air I'd forgotten it was winter. I want to look behind me, catch his watching, but I can't—how does he stop me? Is it some string men fling and hook to your hair; is it this that keeps me steady? Like some bad metaphor, a kite of cold birds rises in concert from a string hung between black poles. Birds are always somebody's soul at crucial moments, but not this moment and the juxtaposition irks—how nature never works. Or never works like you expected, like a book being written about your day or a fluorescent-lined, folding magnifying mirror.

Eurydice in the Underworld

There's less poetry here
than the pales say.
We are oceans suspended
in a clean, deep petal.
You think I want to find
my hands or the man
licked clean by fever.

I want neither. That connection
was long; it made me tired
of bridges forever. Here I can
walk right up to people
and press the length
of their difference. I know you
by hiss and breath of color.
Are we connected?

I cannot remember
impenetrable. Nothing here
is solid. We are laid whole.
That? That slit opens by fire.
A shoulder trying to dim
though. Bodies take
the long way, think
there are troubles for
the reason. I am not separate.

Heat lights quick, needs dark
and time. But I have noise.
I hear Orpheus. Oh music
(it helped me shimmer

into shedding) comes
to wrench me, like he pressed.
Heat! That heavy God,
the constant feet of day,
wound around his marble arm.

The Jackpot

The monogamous are like the very rich. They have to find their poverty. They have to starve themselves enough.
-Adam Philip

We are too flush

our bosky hedge funds
are fecund—
we calculate the slow
growth   the return

but let's try to poormouth
again   I'll be Cinderella
pre-slipper and you
be a cockney starveling

we'll settle
in the slums together
hold struck matches—
our barren grate

won't bloom—
against our fingers
where they have purpled
in December

we'll wolf cold
casseroles of aspic and crackers
afterward   still famished

we'll shake off our
poor white delicates

and glut until surfeited   see

how easy
it can be—the slow slide
soft as
a rummage sale t-shirt—

when you have nothing else
to say   *take me*
into your alms
and mean it?

Congratulations

1.

My rabbit didn't die; it's hidden in
the prickly hedges that no one touches, shivering,
worry running its heart.
                                        I push my mouth
into my pillow and it keeps what I've said
inside its useless pockets. When bread dough
catches in my fingers, we lick them clean

together. The rabbit hops up to our mat
(*Welcome to our Happy Home!*), then skitters
backward, fearing our sudden laughter over
port, your favorite intoxicant, and mine—
something with lemons and bubbles and bursts.

2.

My rabbit is dead; it cannot hide between
the velvet leaves that everyone wants to touch.
It drops down heavy in its skin, the heart
soaked.
            When I settle on a pillow it bursts
sleep and feathers. Bread loaves rise from my hands
when flour stickies between my fingers. Our rabbit's

ghost hops into our hallway, invited by
the silence. We've purchased a plastic chair so it
can join us. You've got your favorite intoxicant—
gin—and I have something dead, like milk, before me.

Back at the Camp

Forced by your
indefatigable push forward to find
more firewood, though the pile
now drives a wedge
into our tent, we go further,
past the line of wasp-waisted
tree-trunks chipped
by beaver teeth. *I bet they're*
making something, you say,
or I say, sounding that airy
conversation that billows unbidden
when people know too much
about each other.
Some of the chipped
trees seem to lean on their skinny, kissing tips.
Everything is soaked and growing
greens and slicks. We find one good,
dead trunk between the furred,
green grasp of a vine.
We untwine the living
thing from what it has sucked
and bent and grown into
the groove. We fall on our asses
as we snap the live fingers back
and extract the light, dry length.
We haul it to the camp and crack
it into pieces. *There'd be*
more, you say,
if we went farther in, but I take
you by the shoulders. *Look*
I say, *look how much*
we have already.

A spider descends
from somewhere above and shivers
across your shoulder. I smash it
with an apple. We are both
staring with concentration
in opposite directions.

Landscape

Our story is broken only
when the tent preachers land,
giving grandma a use for that fancy fan,
making all the bad women
vomit up money. Otherwise, I spend
most days pulling ribbon from the kitten's
belly. Sometimes the husband
takes up hobbies, like disassembling
radios, and scatters the wire-furred
pieces on every empty surface.
I hammered one of his stray dials
to the cupboard and now
I can imagine the creamed corn
talking to me without
looking crazy. I tuck away
the hope that this is just
an independent movie—
the bad teeth bleach clean,
spackled pockmarks peel.
Times like these, the idea
of children plays double-duty
as wish and shiver. They never work,
but people keep making them anyway,
like hand-held sewing machines
and herbal lozenges. Even the lawn,
sun struck mid-summer, wants to die
a little quicker but can find nowhere
high enough to jump from.

I reach my hand inside his cranium,

knock over the chiffon coppice
in his snowglobe, those filaments
of microclimate. I black a whole
constellation—he opens his mouth

and the words fall out backwards. I feed
on rows of yews, their branches withering
upon exposure. Hurry! He's doing the robot

by the doughnut table. I get my momentum
as he crashes the peristyle for pies. I am larger
and more powerful than these errors, but I promise,
I'll stop when my weather bird changes. Soon,

I'll need something to plug up this humming hollow.

Circumstances

If only I could extend the unself
humming when my hands fold and stack,
fold and stack unthinking. If only we could shovel
snow banks from our porch steps. If only I had
a room of yellow spaces, empty of all
superfluity in the form of curtain ruffles,
knick-knacks or framed pictures.
If only it could be caught and recorded
without waking. If only I could drive
out this cold, film at the floor
of my throat, while still tolerable and low-lying.
If only our sheets were always
clean, yellow-smelling and pooled
with cold sun. Then you'd come home
with a bag full of freshly dead salmon
and vine tomatoes. Then the telephone
would never start screaming. Then
we would both be miraculously hungry by seven.

Unlikely

When I cut the chicken's breast
a blood bloom gullies
in the fibers—an un-drained
vein, a popped clot

of live body buried
inside it. Oh, and how
the bicycling student's arm
cracking in half on a coming car's

bright bumper sounds just like
Thanksgiving, when father found
the turkey's Y bone inside
and made me wish.

And how we both,
as children, saw a documentary
about Bonobo monkeys. It went
like this: A baby monkey

coughs then stiffens and falls
from a tree. The mother presses
its dead weight against her chest.
The others scatter, fearing the odor
after two weeks, five, then ten, and then
the baby's bones and skin fall unbidden
from her body. How unlikely,

you observe, avoiding the ribbon
I've opened, the surprising black
abundance, that we both took

this knowledge almost together,
at the same exact moment.

Out Like a Lamb

It's only the usual signs:
the tree dumping sticky
seed all over
the windshield, hedges pelting

pink flowers when its arms
are arched
then released
by the wind in an oohing
snap back,

froth, and the yeast's
ferment burping
in the bucket. It's time

to bottle, and the bottles
swell till the plastic cracks, corks
fat, caps threaten to
unscrew when you touch them.

It needs at least nine
months until done. Meanwhile,
everything we own is soaked

in clove and old honey and
the air's so thick it zips—the pressure
might rip my skin. Outside,

the wind picks up
a real estate sign and sends
it through the neighbor's

picture window. Hail clots
the roadside gutters and shatters
all of their favorite baby pictures.

Definitional #1

One who has produced
something, a plant bearing
a glossy red or green fruit,
a heavy axe,
in its original state, the fruit itself,
good for eating, alert and knowing
a formidable woman,
one who is sexually desired,
a person who lowers his standards
for profit, not made use of, sly,
slang for an enormous
ocean liner, a woman who gives
birth to a child, witty,
reddish in color, a woman
who engages in sexual acts
for profit, any of numerous
mouse-like mammals
of nondescript color, processed
or worked for the first time,
implicating *limp-wristed*, a part
of female genitalia,
unbroken earth, a scolding
woman, one who is sought
and never captured.

The Trouble

I’ve stilled the house
completely. I hear blood
whirring, its sound like the sound
of the mother’s heart
crowding the infant’s ear.

Nothing out gets in unless
I ask, unless I want to skitter
the roll of regular, the daily
punctuation of my sky
with one perfect bird.

A man paces my green
lawn in a tuxedo. I raise
his hand and make him wave,
make his face fall. The bird
beats from my frame,
scenting a storm’s arrival.

If I could find that hammer
the curved end for prying
up nails and floorboards, I might
slip through the window.
I might give him my umbrella.

Give

It always sounds sad
to give up or in or out. Always
sad, climbing into somebody else's

disheveled bed. Can't sleep
though you can't do anything else
and the car wheels' splats

sound through the glass. So it's
supposed to mean collapsed. Burst
spokes and popping your filling

in a caramel apple. Too many
mouthfuls and now you can't
do without them. It's supposed

to be sad to give up,
though there's that good sag and drop.
And sighs

are like that— out, and out,
like getting home late
from work

and easing the tight, laced shoes off,
falling down into the crumby,
change clanking couch.

Supposed to be sad, to give up, or
in, or out, but I say
                                        what about
the cardinal virtue

of benevolence? I'll give
you my hat, my skirt, my shirt,
my stockings, my salty

and sweet delicates and
then my hand if you'll give
me a good, ballooning below
me, place to drop.

Notes

The poems in section two all use sentences and pieces of sentences from the 1982 version of the *Reader's Digest Guide to North American Wildlife*. Some of these poems come from applying the N+7 OULIPO method to the text, some use other OULIPO methods, and some are collages or cut-ups.

BIOGRAPHY

Letitia Trent's work has appeared in the D*enver Quarterly, The Black Warrior Review, Fence, Folio, The Journal, Mipoesias, Ootoliths, Blazevox*, and many others. Her chapbooks include *Splice* (Blue Hour Press), *The Medical Diaries* (Scantily Clad Press), and *You aren't in this movie* (dancing girl press).

Trent was the 2010 winner of the Alumni Flash Writing Award from the Ohio State University's *The Journal* and has been awarded fellowships from The Vermont Studio Center and the MacDowell Colony.

SUNDRESS PUBLICATIONS TITLES

The Bone Folders
T.A. Noonan
$14.95 ISBN 0-9723224-6-9

Like a Fish
Daniel Crocker
$14.95 ISBN 0-9723224-8-5

Especially the Deer
Tyurina Allen, Mary Beth Magin,
& Julie Ruble
$12.99 ISBN 0-9723224-0-X

www.ingramcontent.com/pod-product-compliance
Ingram Content Group UK Ltd.
Pitfield, Milton Keynes, MK11 3LW, UK
UKHW040557210726
13854UKWH00008B/1382